WHO STARTED THE UNITED FARM WORKERS UNION?

The Story of Cesar Chavez

Biography of Famous People

Children's Biography Books

BABY PROFESSOR

EDUCATION KIDS

César Chavez spent thirty years working on behalf of migrant farm workers in the United States. Why did he do that, and what did he do? Let's take a look!

EARLY DAYS

César Chavez was born in 1927 in Arizona. His parents were from Mexico and owned a grocery store and a farm. But they lost everything in the Great Depression, which started in 1929. Chavez's father had to go to work as a farm laborer, and the family moved to California.

The "Dustbowl" During The Great Depression

As he grew up, Chavez moved up and down the state with his family, in very hard conditions. The camps migrant laborers lived in were primitive, the work was hard, wages were very low, and there was a lot of racism and corrupt practices that hurt the workers and their families.

Whaen he was old enough,
Chavez joined the U.S.
Navy. He spent two years in
the Navy, and then returned
to working on farms to help
his family.

Cesar Chavez Monument

Migrant Workers

WHAT MIGRANT FARM
WORK IS LIKE

W hat is it like to be in a family of migrant farm workers? Things are better than they were, partly because of what César Chavez did, but it is still no picnic!

igrant workers travel from farm to farm, planting or harvesting whatever crop is ready. They live in temporary housing. There are as many as three million farm workers in the U.S., and many of them are migrants. Three-quarters of all farm workers in the United States were born in Mexico.

Migrant Workers

Family of Migrant Workers

Most farm workers are married and have families, but more than half of the men spend a lot of the year away from their families, traveling from farm to farm. Farm workers aren't included in the protections of most federal labor laws. They were excluded from laws protecting their ability to form unions, laws establishing safe working conditions, and laws setting a minimum wage. The minimum wage law was changed in 1978, partly because of Chavez's work, to cover farm workers.

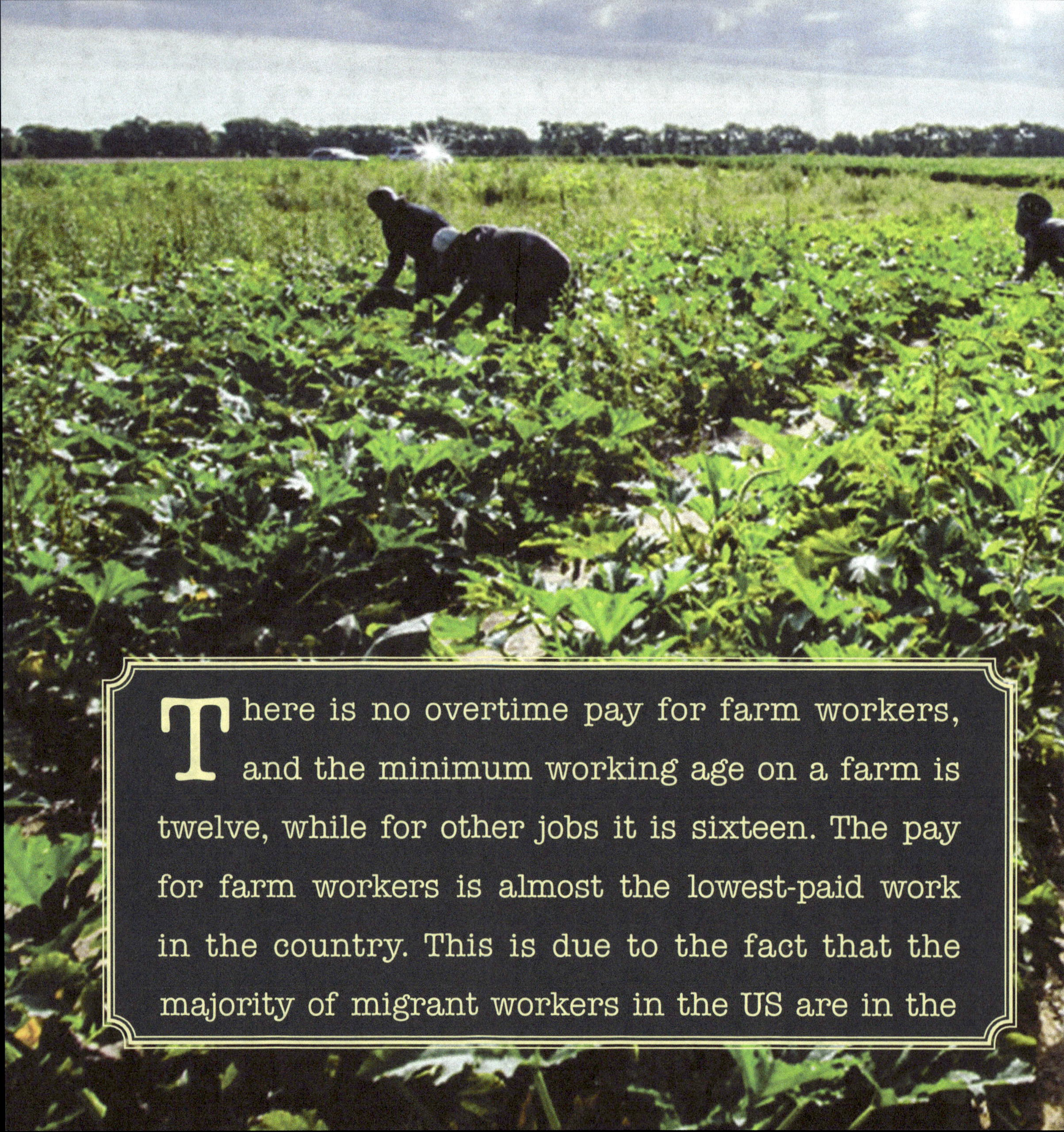

There is no overtime pay for farm workers, and the minimum working age on a farm is twelve, while for other jobs it is sixteen. The pay for farm workers is almost the lowest-paid work in the country. This is due to the fact that the majority of migrant workers in the US are in the

country illegally. Because of this they have no legal grounds to insist on higher wages for their work. Farm work is one of the four most dangerous jobs in the United States, along with logging, commercial fishing, and flying airplanes.

Farm workers suffer the country's worst rate of injuries from toxic chemicals in pesticides. Half of America's farm workers have not completed seventh grade, and over ten percent had less than three years of formal education. This is not because they did not want to learn. Constantly moving from place to place is disruptive to education.

LEARNING TO ORGANIZE

In 1952, when he was 25, Chavez met people who worked to help improve the situation of migrant laborers. Fred Ross, a community organizer, invited Chavez to join the Community Service Organization (CSO).

Cesar Chavez

United Farm Workers

Chavez worked hard and learned well, and within a few years he was the national director of the CSO. But in 1962 he started work on a union for farm workers, and left the CSO to found the Farm Workers Association.

STRUGGLES TO ORGANIZE

Building a farm workers' union was hard. Employers threatened to fire anybody who was involved in the union, and people were scared to lose their jobs. Many farm workers were in the United States illegally, and were afraid of being deported.

Cesar Chavez

Plaza de Cesar Chavez

In 1965, the young union joined the strike in the California grape fields that workers from the Philippines had started. Chavez soon became a leader of the effort.

His work in this strike and in other efforts had some consistent features:

⇒ The struggle is not just about pay checks, but about civil rights issues: dignity, access to health care, fair labor conditions, and ending racial discrimination.

⇒ The struggle is non-violent.

⇒ The effort brought in volunteers from labor and church groups who could add their experiences and help carry the effort with the striking workers.

⇒ The farm workers' effort had to join hands with the efforts of all workers, especially in labor unions.

⇒ Big events, like marches and sit-ins, get public attention. If you get the public on your side, you are closer to winning the strike. A march on the state legislature in Sacramento changed the strike from a local event in some fields to a state-wide or even nation-wide issue.

JUST TIRES

First Headquarters of the United Farm Workers Labor Union

Personal commitment: Chavez went on hunger strikes several times to draw attention to the issues the strike was about. He was willing to put his health and even his life on the line. In 1970, over twenty-five grape-growers in the Delano region agreed to recognize the union and negotiate a contract with the workers. The union had won!

But at the same time the union had to fight on another front. Another union, the Teamsters, also wanted to represent the farm workers. The Teamsters were willing to sign contracts with large farm corporations that were not very good for the workers, but were good for the union.

Striking Teamsters

Farm Workers

Chavez and the United Farm Workers (UFW) fought against the Teamsters' effort, in court and sometimes in physical battles in the fields, until 1973. Finally the Teamsters agreed to not compete with the UFW.

Chavez believed that laws had to be in place to protect and benefit farm workers so they did not have to keep fighting the same issues over and over again. This was a long-term battle with limited success; many large growers resisted any changes to conditions in the fields or rates of pay.

The National Chavez Center

THE GRAPE BOYCOTT

Chavez and the UFW worked for many years to get farmers and growers to use less pesticides on their crops, as they were often toxic to the people who had to work in the fields. The growers resisted making any changes.

In 1984 Chavez called for a world boycott of table grapes grown in California. This was consistent with his efforts over many decades to make the workers' struggles not just a matter of the worker in the field and the owner of the farm. It also involved the people who ate what came from the farm— or chose not to.

Grape Vineyard

Hundreds of farm workers visited cities across the United States and Canada to explain what the strike and boycott were about, and to call for support from people who may never have visited a farm. The boycott grew until almost 20 million Americans had pledged not to eat table grapes until the issue was resolved.

Restaurants around the world removed grapes from their menus. The workers explained to anyone who would listen that the simple act of not eating grapes now could lead to a better life for farm workers in the future.

UNION
JUSTIC
DIGNE
Cesar Chavez

The boycott that began in 1984 went on for sixteen years. The grape growers resisted making changes, but eventually they came to see that their resistance was costing them more in lost sales than the changes would cost them.

F inally the strike and boycott ended in 2000. Grape growers agreed to stop using five toxic pesticides that were harming workers in the fields. It was a great victory for farm workers everywhere, and for the country as a whole.

Cesar Chavez

Cesar Chavez gravesite

Unfortunately, César Chavez did not live to see this victory. His life of hard work, and his many hunger strikes, had weakened his body. He died in 1993 at the age of 66. He had worked for over thirty years to build a movement that would improve the lives of millions of the poorest and most oppressed workers in the United States.

About César Chavez

⇒ Here are some interesting facts about this hard worker for the rights of farm laborers:

⇒ When Chavez was 15, he had to quit school and go to work in the fields full time to help support his family.

⇒ In 1948, when Chavez returned from his military service, he married his long-time sweetheart, Helen Favela. They had eight children.

⇒ Chavez worked hard for civil rights for all Latinos, not just farm workers.

CESAR ESTRADA CHAVEZ
1927 - 1993
Cesar Chavez Grave

Memorial Garden where César Chávez is buried

In 1994, President Bill Clinton awarded the Presidential Medal of Freedom to Chavez in honor of his lifetime of effort to improve the lives of many.

In 2000, the State of California established March 31 as a state holiday to honor Chavez. César Chavez had a motto for all his work: "Sí, se puede." That means, "Yes, it can be done."

Cesar Chavez Memorial

CHOOSE TO DO GOOD,
NOT TO PLAY SAFE

Cesar Chavez dedicated himself to improving the lives of millions of people. He raised the tone of the national conversation about workers' rights, the effects of pesticides and sub-standard pay for migrant workers.

It is hard to choose to do the good thing instead of the safe thing. To read about others who made this choice, try Baby Professor books like Marquis de Lafayette: The Hero of Two Worlds and A Rich Man in Poor Clothes: The Story of Saint Francis of Assisi.

Cesar Chavez

Visit
BABY PROFESSOR
EDUCATION KIDS
www.BabyProfessorBooks.com
to download Free Baby Professor eBooks
and view our catalog of new and exciting
Children's Books